Taylor Made Publishing, LLC
PO Box 861 Greenville, NC 27835
www.taylormadebooks.com

Copyright #
ISBN:
Editor: Jorge L. Hernandez
Printed in USA.

Dedication

This book is dedicated to the loving memory of my father, Robert C. Vaughan.

I love and miss you, Daddy.

Purpose

As you read through the pages of this book, my prayer is that you will be guided by the Holy Spirit, captivated by each line, excited to search and find every word, inspired to create your own beautiful adult coloring pages, and be richly blessed by your experience.

Thank you so much for your support!

Love,
Robbi

God's Gift

Brothers and sisters
Let me tell the story
Of how I was blessed
With the gift of poetry
I often asked God, You see
Oh, Lord, what is my destiny?
Why do I feel so unworthy?
Why have You created me?
You see, I didn't have a purpose or
A reason to live on
My hopes and dream were shattered
Faith and self-esteem were gone
Oh, Lord, I cried, with tears in my eyes
I feel like I'm losing my mind!
God said, "Focus on Me and you will see
Your gift, your season, it's time!"
I thank you for this gift, Lord,
But what am I supposed to do?
He said, "I gave you this special gift,
So, I can speak through you!
Now go, share your poetry, with everyone
In need of inspiration
Poetically you'll make Me proud
For you are My creation!"

God's Gift

Word search is a fun and relaxing way to explore and learn. Have lots of fun searching for the words in the upcoming word search pages of this book after certain poems. Let the word search begin.

```
U S Z J X E M E E T S E F L E S V D
N H T I D R E E D R E A M S O K I E
I A F N V E N L I B O A U Z Q R E S
N T I S R I Y F G W E T R H U L D T
S T G P V E C E Q T Y Z N S G I D I
I E C I P O R T S H O P E S G E U N
G R D R O F E O U L L E T U N I G Y
N E L A E U A S M N Y T H O S M F P
I D O T T S T I C H O E I I Z U Y T
F I R I R E I O T F U T D P T F A Y
I E D O Y O O M S H S E S O P R U P
C Y E N A O N T M E S P E C I A L V
A E N O G R O M U F U V M U U E Z G
N F O J A R E Q J W K D Z W E E E S
T B J B Y V D E I R C Q J D U O R P
```

Faith   Proud   Tears   Story   Gone   Hopes   Divine   Cried
Creation   Poetry   Dreams   Special   Purpose   Shattered
Self-esteem   Inspiration   Questioned   Destiny   Insignificant
Gift   Lord   Lord   Tell   Gift   Eyes

7

Use Me, Lord

Use me, Lord!
To spread joy and hope
A hug or smile
Encourage and uplift
Acknowledge that I am Your child
Letting them know
They will see a brighter day
Trouble don't last forever
Your help is on the way
Use me, Lord!
To break down walls
of confusion
To discern from the devil's
Sinful delusions
To tell them focus on Jesus
He'll give them inner peace
Turn their lives around
While blessings are released
Use me, Lord!
To pray fervently
For unwilling souls
Spreading Your word
So, Your life will be told
Standing firm and unmovable
Walking by faith, not sight
Staying connected to You
Every day and night
Use me, Lord!
Until my days on this earth are complete
And I can hear God say,
"My child, well done,
With Me you will stay
Take My hand and walk with Me
Down these golden streets
To live eternally!"

Use Me, Lord

Use your skills to find all of the words below. Words may appear forwards or backwards, horizontally, vertically or diagonally. Here we go!

```
Q  C  H  F  H  U  G  G  E  F  F  S  I  G  H  T  R  O
Y  O  J  B  I  N  E  M  P  M  S  M  I  L  E  B  E  W
E  Z  C  L  O  W  U  L  F  E  E  C  A  E  P  O  V  U
I  O  O  E  A  R  E  R  E  A  U  I  U  F  O  V  E  K
D  D  N  S  T  H  Q  L  P  P  I  M  S  E  S  O  R  M
D  U  F  S  R  C  S  O  U  G  O  T  T  I  B  A  O  O
E  N  U  I  O  U  V  R  E  Y  N  H  H  R  N  Y  F  S
S  W  S  N  U  V  Q  D  L  S  F  I  I  I  P  F  N  E
A  I  I  G  B  D  P  T  S  L  O  G  K  I  P  O  U  N
E  L  O  S  L  V  N  G  I  L  H  U  Y  L  I  K  V  L
L  L  N  D  E  E  D  G  N  T  L  A  L  S  A  E  D  I
E  I  O  M  V  A  O  W  E  M  R  E  U  S  E  W  O  F
R  N  W  R  Y  I  C  R  C  P  E  L  W  B  K  Z  E  M
E  G  E  N  Q  D  W  O  L  O  E  M  E  I  K  G  A  C
S  F  A  O  G  H  S  W  L  D  U  C  U  C  Q  I  O  I
```

Released   Delusions   Confusion   Fervently   Blessings
Unwilling   Peace   Brighter   Trouble   Walking   Forever
Sight   Faith   Hope   Smile   Done   Souls   Help   Sinful
Me   Hug   Use   Day   Pray   Joy   Well   Lord

9

I AM

I AM the voice who calms your fears
I AM comfort for your tears
I AM a friend on a rainy day
I AM the light to guide your way
I AM medicine to ease your pain
I AM the sun after the rain
I AM shelter from the storm
I AM joy in the morn
I AM a rock for you to stand
I AM the one who holds your hand
I AM patience, hope, and love
I AM blessing you from above
I AM alpha and omega
I AM God,
The Almighty Creator!

JESUS

JESUS
Son of God
Child of Mary
Born unto this world
Our sins to carry
Preaching and teaching
Healing bodies and souls
To sacrifice His life
Was the ultimate goal
Taking on the sins
Of a corrupt world
Suffering lash after lash
For every man, woman,
Boy and girl
Torture unimaginable
Unbearable pain
Nailed to that old rugged cross
And knowing we would sin again
He gave up His life
For sin and salvation
While meditating on
His Father's revelation
But the good news is
He was not defeated
He arose from the tomb
His mission completed
Born unto this world
Eternal life, He gives
Resurrected and connected
Our Savior lives
Jesus, Jesus, Jesus!

Jesus

You will truly find Jesus as you search for these words.

```
N B T C A U R U Z L A Q I M T D Y I
T O O O O O R U O E O S E E M U N R
G O I L I R H R E V E L A T I O N S
N S M T A X R U O V H E A L I N G U
I J A B A S N U I S A C R I F I C E
H B U V I V A L P J Y E U P C B O A
C T I N I X L R D T A N F O C E T E
A L S C D O N A O M I I N P A A E R
E M A I O N R D S S R N I S E L A U
R E F N G O Y T X I E F Z M I N C T
P C S I R S Y I J C F Y S F Y R H R
M B S U S E J O T I T L E S M O I O
A A H W W C T E R E H T A F O B N T
L I R C U L D E D E N P T F R G O
M T D Y R E S U R R E C T E D I C Z
```

Jesus   Mary   Tomb   Lives   Savior   Arose   Father   Cross
Revelation   Teaching   Preaching   Resurrected   Connected
Torture   Corrupt   Salvation   Sacrifice   Eternal   Healing
Our   Life   God   Son   Born   Sins

13

Didn't You Know:
A Message from God

Didn't you know?
You mean the world to Me
I gave My only son
So you could be free!
Didn't you know?
If you pray fervently
I'll give you abundant blessings
And spiritual harmony!
Didn't you know?
Trials are going to come
But if you just trust in Me
Your victory will be won!
Didn't you know?
If you call on My holy name
Accept Me into your heart
You will never be the same
Ever again!

Lazarus, Come Forth

Can you imagine?
A man buried four days
In a tomb sealed by a stone
His sisters and friends
Thought he was dead
And his soul to glory went on
Now enter a man named Jesus
Guided by God's direction
He said, "Move that stone,
Lazarus, come forth!"
Come forth for your resurrection
Now if you don't believe in miracles
Lazarus is a witness you see
Jesus can perform miracles in your life
Believing and accepting Him is the key
He will encourage you in spirit
When you feel like giving up
When you're down and empty
He will fill your cup
He will give you peace
That others don't understand
He will guide you
And hold your hand
So, turn your problems over to Jesus
Let Him be your forever decree
Because He waits with open arms
To set your spirit free!

Lazarus, Come Forth

Rise up and see how many words you can find.

```
I  S  A  D  E  A  S  J  C  U  A  K  M  E  N  O  A  X
F  W  G  T  S  C  J  E  M  L  Y  V  Z  Y  A  P  H  I
M  Z  S  W  J  T  B  E  L  I  E  V  I  N  G  R  S  A
V  B  O  I  Z  L  I  W  F  C  R  U  C  O  Q  O  I  T
U  N  D  E  R  S  T  A  N  D  A  A  Y  E  A  B  W  O
I  M  A  G  I  N  E  F  W  T  E  R  C  J  C  L  I  H
R  E  S  U  R  R  E  C  T  I  O  N  I  L  C  E  T  T
D  N  A  H  S  J  F  G  E  T  O  M  B  M  E  M  N  I
D  X  C  P  E  E  W  U  P  U  Z  R  F  E  P  S  E  R
E  C  S  M  E  S  J  Y  Y  E  E  U  R  N  T  F  S  I
L  A  Z  A  R  U  S  M  R  R  R  N  E  O  I  Y  S  P
A  T  A  P  C  S  S  O  U  L  O  F  E  T  N  V  E  S
E  C  O  U  E  D  E  I  R  U  B  L  O  S  G  A  Y  Y
S  E  M  P  D  R  A  I  S  E  R  E  G  R  C  P  X  T
T  V  R  K  A  Y  A  X  E  O  O  S  J  E  M  C  F  J
```

Sealed   Buried   Tomb   Decree   Peace   Stone   Jesus
Understand   Believing   Accepting   Resurrection   Problems
Lazarus   Witness   Miracles   Imagine   Miracles   Perform
Spirit   Soul   Glory   Raise   Waits   Hand   Free

17

Throne of Grace

Throne of Grace
Peace, tranquility,
God's blessings,
Are all in this place
Come, let Me lead you to
The throne of grace
Sisters and brothers
Bonding in unity
No hate, no war
Just sweet harmony
Behold the majesty of Jesus' face
Come on,
Let Me take you to
The throne of grace
Heartache and pain are no longer there
No worries, no stress
No troubles, no fear
Close your eyes to be surrounded by
The comfort of the Lord
Meditate and appreciate
Your faith being restored
Think not on your finances
Nor stress from the day
Just listen softly
To hear what God has to say
As you pray your stress away
Know that God hears you
Tomorrow is a better day
He will see you through
Now rejoice and receive
Divine healing in this place
Oh, what joy there is at
The throne of grace!

Can I Get an Amen?

What's wrong with people these days?
They won't even give God some praise
Ashamed to open their mouths
And shout, "Thank you, Lord!"
Sitting in church, stiff as a board
So many caught up in life's
Twists and turns
Worrying about the next dollar they'll earn
Robbing Peter to pay Paul
They need a holy wake-up call!
Some sit on pompous pedestals of pride
With their lips pressed tightly
Trying to hide
The pain inside from years ago
What's wrong with them?
Don't they know!
That God can give them joy again
If they only let Him in
Heart, mind, body and soul
For the truth must be told
Come down off that
Pedestal of pride
Because from God
They'll never hide
It's time to stop pretending
And start surrendering
For God's love
Is never ending
He'll turn pride into praise
The spiritually dead
He will raise
Up to exalt
His wonderful name
To praise Him for real
Not shout for fame
Better get on that worship train
In the sunshine or in the rain
Give God your whole heart
Don't wait until the end…
Brothers and sisters,
Can I Get an Amen?!

It's Tight but It's Right

It's tight but it's right
Put on that armor, sword, and shield
Time to stand
Time to fight!
For the devil is busy
In this wicked world
Searching for souls
Men, women, boys, and girls!
Anyone he can possess
Using drugs, violence, lust, and hate
Calling on his deceitful demons
To destroy and devastate!
Open up your eyes
It's time to realize
Don't fall into his trap
Don't feed into his lies!
Seek ye first the kingdom of God and
His righteousness
Accept Jesus' marvelous light
Chose the road to Heaven or hell today
It's tight but it's right!

It's Tight but It's Right

Let's tighten up and find the words below.

```
O O R I G H T E O U S N E S S F V H
Y A X T O X K S A U Q Q A D Z X H M
P E E Y T C Z M U N G D L O O O A E
T C T N O I E X S L E R W I C K E D
O N A T H G I T F S O D L B D X T C
Y E T F I G H T T W R I R E R N A H
X L S P D I F R L O G S E X U E H R
H O A E E I O U H U R W Z G V R P
U I V P V Y Q S T O U S K K S A I T
S V E I I F J I L W S E I D A E G O
H N D C L E O E C E E N L L E H H Z
I F E Z S I V U S S G B U E I D T A
E P C U T R C S N D J R U A R M O R
L I S U A C O W O N E D T O U X O U
D R H M K P D M G T U U S E C G O D
```

Devastate Kingdom Violence Marvelous Righteousness
World Fight Armor Drugs Seek Right Jesus Devil
Tight Shield Destroy Sword Possess Heaven Wicked
Light Lust Hell God Hate

23

It's Not about You

It's not about you
But the Holy Spirit who dwells inside
Giving divine instructions
Appointed to be your guide
Are you walking and talking with Jesus?
Experiencing the overflow
Rebuking weapons formed against you
Telling that devil, "No!"
Remember, it's not about you
Nor the kind of clothes you wear
Not even the money you have
But the love that we must share
Keep your mind stayed on Jesus
For He saved our sinful souls
Then offered us the invitation
To walk down streets of gold
Brothers and sisters,
Listen to His voice
Lead with honor and integrity
Digest the fruits of the spirit
And stand firm against the enemy
Let us all follow Jesus
So when our journey is through
God will say, "Well Done,
My good and faithful servant,
I welcome you!"

It's Not about You

It's all about you searching and finding the words below.

```
W E A P O N S A V I L V T U O B A H
A B E P C D O D G U I D E O G E L G
K D E H D L O G O D X Q W K U U E I
G N I K L A W S A N F A S L F U D N
G N I K U B E R P I E F G H A R W S
D E T N I O P P A I E O T A N L E T
S E R V A N T A I Y R I O T I F L R
F O V E R F L O W M A I M T A N L U
C O F D S E M S I F B R T A F D S C
N Y R L E N S T R E E T S L E S U T
T W U M M V O U L Y O N K K Y H L I
A O E P E F I T E E N I V I D G Y O
S R S L H D N L U F N I S N F Z O N
O K E N L E T S T I U R F G B E U S
E D F F E N R H A T C D C H E P O A
```

Against   Walking   Faithful   Formed   Talking   Servant
Streets   Not   Souls   Divine   Sinful   Dwells   Guide   About
Rebuking   Overflow   Appointed   Weapons   Instructions
You   Devil   Well   Gold   Done   Fruits   Spirit

The Storms

Raging through your life
Bringing strong winds of despair
Sending thunderous clouds of desperation
Satan is in the air
Whirling into your thoughts
Thoughts of no return
Blinded by the darkness
He wants you to burn
Still these storms keep raging
Raging like never before
To seek out the weak ones
Can you hear Satan's roar?
Negative thoughts enter your mind
You're close to breaking down
He thinks that he has won, then
You feel God's presence all around
Just when you felt like giving up
For those storms are too hard to bear
Look around for the eye of Jesus
You'll find your peace, right there!

The Storms

Find the peace in your storms as you search the word list below

```
R E Y N A R J T R S A E Q R E N F C
V I R X L Y N E C A I E P M K D B M
E P A E S E N O S S P R F A I C G E
G F S P H D Y W D U E D E T D T E P
U S N H S T X U M S S W T A Z V D W
F I A A O E O U E A Z R R I Y E M M
D N I F T L D N B P B K W T L C S J
F E S F C A C N E L N E A I A D P T
A E M I J E S A R E I G Y Q R R E H
K D R D E T C N S U E N I E O A R G
C N O U C E D S I N U J D C U H A I
C M T H U N D E R O U S B E N E T R
R G S T H G U O H T E F L U D A I O
O O L I F E H O G N I G A R R M O W
Z D N O P U A C P R A E B C E N N I
```

Presence   Thoughts   Desperation   Darkness   Thunderous
Weak   There   Satan   Jesus   Clouds   Ones   Peace   Find
Storms   Despair   Around   Blinded   Negative   Raging
God   Right   Burn   Eye   Life   Hard   Bear

Spiritual Cleansing

Spiritual frustration
Devastation
Hopes and dreams shattered
My soul is battered
Just want to give up
Don't feel like pressing on
God speaks, "The battle is not yours,
It's Mine, so stay strong!"
But the walls are caving in, Lord
I feel like I'm going to explode
The weight of the world is on my shoulders
Please take away this heavy load.
God says, "My child, cry out to Me
Let your tears flow like rain
Renew your spirituality
Cleanse away all of your pain
Give it all to Me
So you can be free
To walk in your destiny
Just sit back and watch
Your blessings unfold
My faithful, beautiful child
Cleansing is good for the soul!"

Prayer Warriors

Covered by Jesus' blood
Bible tightly in hand
Led by the Holy Spirit
Prayer warriors, stand!
Wearing the full armor
Breastplate, sword, and shield
Knowing that in this battle
We must not yield!
For the devil is busy
Shooting worldly ammunition
Bringing chaos and confusion
Despair and affliction!
But warriors have the power
To crush the devil's plan
Claiming the victory in Jesus' name
Knowing God holds us in His hand!

Rejuvenation

Rejuvenation
Sweet meditation
Jesus' arms all around you
Spiritual relaxation
Rejuvenation
Mind alteration
Step out of the box
To receive this revelation
Rejuvenation
Satan's temptation
He cannot steal your joy
God's affirmation
Rejuvenation
God's irrigation
Washed by the blood,
Born again in Christ,
Blessed by His Salvation!

Watch God Work

Watch God work
In your situation
Erasing the memory
Of your devastation
Giving you a new step
A new praise
A new song
Teaching you to lean
On His everlasting arms
Molding and shaping
Miraculously
Into the divine person
He called you to be
Showered by His love
Grace and mercy, too
Revealing in His word
If you ask, He will do
He will bless you abundantly
Give you the victory
Just open your eyes
You will see…
Watch God work!

Watch God Work

Seek God in the words below and you will definitely find him.

```
O K S E H E B I Q D A C O I A S E O Z
R X D A U D K K U E K R O W S T T G H
P O R M D E V A S T A T I O N U T N F
U M F P I R E V E A L I N G O L B I R
S S O G P R S Y A O Z E A Z R I I R Y
I R D E N K A A N R T G R A C E E E J
A Y E M O I T C W A T C H P E T S W U
D M C U N S D P U D I W A Z B C A O L
G G E R P X J L R L X O H E N C K H R
N N U M E E S O O O M O F A Q V S S
I I O D O M W E Y M D U Z L E N C Y C
H P B T P R A I S E R H S O L O Y G G
C A L I E O Y S R O I T R L V S O G S
A H E E V E R L A S T I N G Y R N N A
E S S E U C V I C T O R Y T E E D O G
T U S A I S I T U A T I O N N P H S F
```

Grace Bless Watch Word Mercy Song Victory Praise
Person Memory Situation Revealing Shaping Molding
Everlasting Teaching Showering Miraculously Devastation
God Lean Arms Work Step

35

God's Got Your Back

Through the doubt
Through the fear
Through the heartache
Through the tears
God's got your back!
When Satan tries to invade your mind
God will step in
Right on time
When you're down and feeling low
He will show you where to go
God's got your back!
No more worries, no more stress
Know that you are eternally blessed
Speak boldly to the enemy,
Tell Him, "I can do all things through Christ
Who strengthens me!"
You're too blessed to be stressed
Be about your Heavenly Father's business
And when the enemy tries to attack
Just remember, God's got your back!

God's Got Your Back

God's got your back in this word search. Seek and you shall find.

```
E U S P E D I E N D U R E S M A
T E A R S E D M O R N I N G R R
S A T C G A T C C O M E S T K U
T N A D V P I F Y C W E I H L O
R T N N M A M E P E O R H G B Y
E H I C R I E T E Q N E D I A U
N G N R M I N P B L A O I N C T
G I O X Z N I D I R U G O D K S
T R E U P N O G T B L G S J W I
H Y O H G S H A T I C Z A R U R
E F E A R T C N B E D D F M J H
N O O S A H M P C I C S M I O C
S B O T E Q D I D T X U S T Y L
```

Doubt Invade Endure Satan Tears Comes
Morning Heartache Weeping Strengthens
Night Right Christ Light Back Mind Time
Joy Fear God On Your

Brothers in Christ

Brothers in Christ
Can I talk to you?
I see the trials
You're going through
I've heard it said
A good man is hard to find
Because the devil can't wait
To take over your mind
You are the glue
That holds the family's bond
Your journey may be rough
But you must press on
And when daggers aimed at you
Are filled with Satan's fire
My brother, stand firm
Tell that devil
He is a liar
Let him know you are blessed
Not stressed
Not depressed
And your soul is possessed
By God's holiness!

Brothers in Christ

Brothers, and sisters also, can search for the words below.

```
H D D H P N J N X E Y U I E D J T
I Y L W L I V E D G L U E P P C A
S E O G N I O G H B R O T H E R S
S N H C K O D O S A S W E D P M U
P R J F B D L Y N O R M E A N I E
D U E I I I N P A S U D M A T I A
E O D G N N S O M Y T L M R S F M
P J U E G T D F B R E A R I I A G
R E S E A A V G I V F H I P R M O
E S K N L P D A I M J Q F M H I O
S V D M I L L P R R I J D T C L D
S R T S A S N T H R O U G H G Y R
E R I F R D E S S E S S O P S X P
D I H M W J E H U C U I T R L I C
```

Good Going Christ Family Stand Through Journey
Devil Trials Bond Soul Glue Mind Hold Hard
Possessed Holiness Depressed Daggers Brothers
Firm Liar Fire Man Find

My Brother

Come here, my brother
Why do I see pain in your eyes?
Is your life all messed up?
Are you listening to Satan's lies?
He wants you in these streets
Selling drugs night after night
Strapped and ready to snap
Just waiting for a reason to fight
Why are you so depressed?
Burdened, broken, and bruised
My brother, give it all to Jesus
You still can be used
Used for God's own glory
Just put your life in His hands
He will take away your pain
Give you a divine plan
He'll take you off these streets
Change your situation
Renew your troubled mind
To receive His revelation
Are you ready for a change?
Tired of living this way
Well, stretch your hands toward Heaven
And just simply say:
Lord, I am a sinner
Please come into my life today
I know You died on the cross for me
So my sins would be washed away
I want to do Your will, Lord
To read and study Your word
Share the joy with everyone
So your story will be heard
Hallelujah, you are saved!
By God's grace and mercy
Now praise His holy name
My brother, you are set free!

My Brother

Search the words below to find your breakthrough.

```
R E Y N A R J T R S A E Q R E N F C
V I R X L Y N E C A I E P M K D B M
E P A E S E N O S S P R F A I C G E
G F S P H D Y W D U E D E T D T E P
U S N H S T X U M S S W T A Z V D W
F I A A O E O U E A E Z R R I Y E M
D N I F T L D N B P B K W T L C S J
F E S F C A C N E L N E A I A D P T
A E M I J E S A R E I G Y Q R R E H
K D R D E T C N S U E N I E O A R G
C N O U C E D S I N U J D C U H A I
C M T H U N D E R O U S B E N E T R
R G S T H G U O H T E F L U D A I O
O O L I F E H O G N I G A R R M O W
Z D N O P U A C P R A E B C E N N I
```

Presence   Thoughts   Desperation   Darkness   Thunderous
Weak   There   Satan   Jesus   Clouds   Ones   Peace   Find
Storms   Despair   Around   Blinded   Negative   Raging
God   Right   Burn   Eye   Life   Hard   Bear

41

Baby Girl

Stop crying
Over broken-hearted pain
Wondering if the sun
Will ever shine again
Burdens on the left
Temptations on the right
Strap on your battle gear
And fight the good fight
Oh no, life is not easy
For that evil enemy
Encourages confusion
Promotes negativity
You say to yourself,
Lord, why me?
The Lord says, "Why not,
This is your destiny!
I'm preparing you
For this mighty war
To stand firm against the devil
Like you've never before
And in the midst of the battle
I will be with you
Transforming your situation
Get ready for a breakthrough
You'll receive salvation
Abundant blessings will overflow
Just hold on, Baby Girl
Don't let go!
Hold on a little longer
Weeping endures for a night
But joy will come in the morning
So, don't give up the fight!"

You Are Blessed

Woman
I feel your pain
Praying to God
Renew my strength again
For sometimes this battle
Put your faith to the test
Be not discouraged
You Are Blessed
Woman
I hear you crying
Filled with heartache
There's no denying
Popping pills for depression
Headaches or stress
Turn it over to Jesus
You Are Blessed
Woman
I see you praising the Lord
Holding tight to that Bible
Like a mighty sword
Knowing God is there
In the midst of it all
And He'll pick you up
When you start to fall
Woman
God will open closed doors
And give you success
You are strong
You are beautiful
You are intelligent
You Are Blessed!

I Am Woman

I am meek and mild
Bold and vivacious
Outspoken and daring
Caring and courageous
I pray to my omnipotent
Heavenly Father above
Fueled by the Holy Spirit
Guided by His love
As I press toward the mark
A little each day
I'm on the battlefield
And for my Lord I'll stand
So, devil get out of my way
Because I'm in God's hand
Now you ask who I am
What motivates me
And how I can smile
Through adversity
I was formed from the rib of man
God's miraculous creation
Still praising, still raising
The next generation
You see,
It was on the solid rock
I built my foundation
While leaning and depending on Jesus
Blessed with salvation
I am destined for greatness
Encouraged and set free
Led by the Holy Spirit
I'll tell you my identity
I Am Woman
And so proud to be!

I Am Woman

Find all of the words below as you celebrate all women.

```
C O U R A G E O U S C D V E U E M C L
U Q L M S P I R I T N W F L S Y I Q A
P C A A E K I K N P R A Y L L E R U C
A A D V E R S I T Y W R O O C L A O E
T U H S I R W K E E M V H Q I Z C Y I
T V A D E D I U G O E C C V D Y U E D
G T K T C G B L R G S D E I L L L Y L
D L E I F E L T T A B D J N T S O A I
D R O M N I P O T E N T E F E B U B M
I R O R O U Y O E N H V A W E Q S K F
Y D R L C A R I N G A T M W D O R P U
P R A I S I N G O E H M O T I V A T E
I R A I S I N G H E N O I T A E R C L
U O P H R R N E R O W P A I I T S I E
R D K E U G A N J V I V A C I O U S D
N O I T A R E N E G B E F C P O V K O
```

Omnipotent Generation Miraculous Courageous Battlefield
Spirit Raising Meek Fueled Father Devil Guided Caring
Motivate Creation Praising Vivacious Heavenly Adversity
Lord Bold Pray Love Mild Holy

Mother-to-Be

First conceiving
Then believing
Knowing that God
Is still achieving
Planting the seed
Child of God indeed
Blessing and soothing
Growing and moving
Mother-to-be
Claim the victory
Pray faithfully
And fervently
Until the finale
Your baby born
Healthy and strong
Showered with love
From God above
So, whether surgery date
Or water break
Mother-to-be
Claim the victory!

Single Sista

Single Sista
Sanctified Sista
Praying to God fervently
To send you a virtuous man
Rooted and grounded in thee
Single Sista
Patient Sista
Looking up to God above
To help you fight
Against fleshy desires
As He covers you with His love
Single Sista
Careful Sista
Been hurt by those frogs before
They never turned in to princes
Just walked right out the door
Single Sista
Blessed Sista
Get ready to shout and sing
For God will send you a blessing
Not a prince but a virtuous king!

Divine Destiny

My spouse
My lover
My soul mate
I've discovered
That you and I
Were meant to be
We were blessed by
Divine destiny
As my love for you
Grows stronger each day
I thank the Lord
For sending you my way
I promise to be your best friend
Hold you in my arms
When you're feeling blue
Communicate and appreciate
The wonderful things you do
And yes, I truly believe
God made you just for me
For we are a match made in Heaven
Blessed by divine destiny!

Love

I am the greatest
I'll never fail
You can't buy me
I'm not for sale
I am a blessing to give
Each day of the week
My actions are genuine
I pray before I speak
I'll mend broken relationships
Bond families together
I am that true friend
In any kind of weather
I work well with faith
Hope and patience, too
I won't anger or hate
Forgive is what I do
I am not jealous
Nor filled with evil pride
My focus is on Jesus
In Him I will abide
My name is love
Just put me to the test
Keep me in your life
And God will do the rest!

Blessed Educator

Excited Educator
Student motivator
Leading by positivity
Genuine personality
Keeping it real
So they can see
That their past doesn't dictate
What their future will be
Loving Educator
Mind cultivator
Sharing the knowledge of yesterday
Building the bridge
Paving the way
Leading them toward the
Road called success
Claiming that they are blessed by the best
Blessed Educator
You are their elevator
Helping them embrace
Their education
Preparing them for graduation
Rewarded by fist bumps, hugs, and smiles
Excited you went that extra mile
We thank God, the Almighty Creator
For our blessed educators!

Elevate Your Mind

Elevate your mind
It's time
For graduation
Means separation
From youth to adulthood
Sometimes being misunderstood
See, time will suddenly create
An excited graduate
Filled with hopes and dreams
Joining the real-world scene
Know that faith determines your destiny
So, think and act positively
Elevate your mind
It's time
To stand firm against the enemy
Believing Jesus is the key
To unlock that door called success
Keeping you uplifted and blessed
Focus on Jesus Christ
Because He made the sacrifice
He died for you and me
So we could be set free
He'll calm your inner fears
Wipe away your weary tears
He'll give you perfect peace
And make your joy increase
Elevate your mind
It's time
Graduate, be encouraged
Don't be discouraged
Know that you are blessed
By the Almighty best
Keep Christ forever in your heard
And let God do the rest!

HIStory...

That old rugged cross
The awful pain
He did bear
Hung, bled, and died for us
Showing and proving that He cared
Holding the weight of all our sins
With nails deep in His hands
So we would follow Him
And truly understand
His story is like no other
The ultimate sacrifice
Sent by God, the Father
To lay down His life
When we celebrate our history
We must remember His story
His grace and mercy
His honor and glory
Oh yes, Jesus loves us
More than we'll ever know
We are covered by His blood
Everywhere we go
Let's celebrate Jesus Christ
For us, he gave His life
And when our time on Earth is over
We will meet Him in paradise!

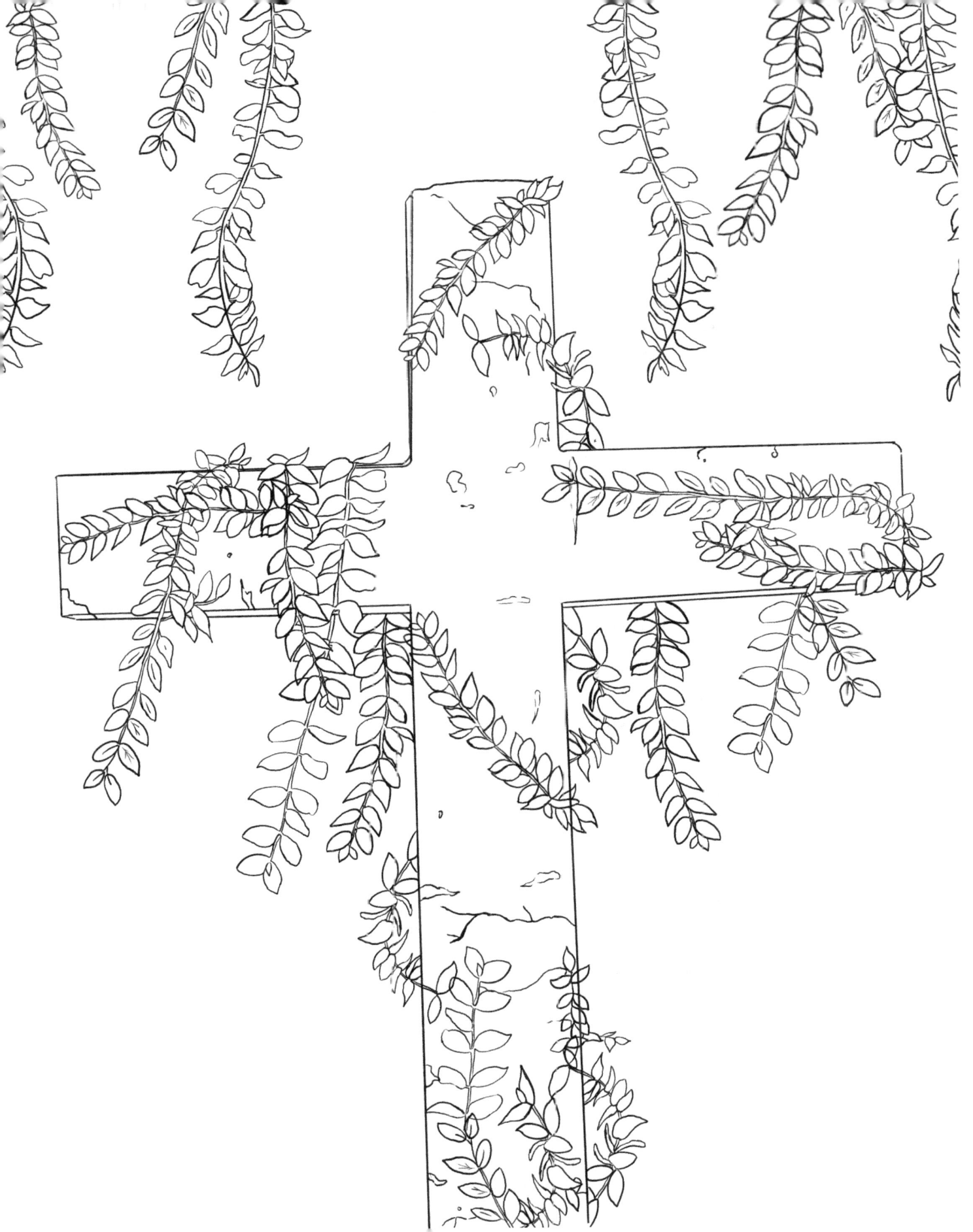

Nubian Eyes

Nubian Eyes
Tell your story
Of struggle, of pain
Of hope, of glory
Shedding sad soulful tears
Of a mistreated race
While searching the heavens
For God's saving grace
Then God poured out a blessing
So those tear-filled eyes could see
He said the storm is over
My child you've been set free
Freed from the pain
Of Masta's whip
The sweet taste of freedom
He'll graciously sip
Shouting, glory hallelujah
No more chains holding me
Then they march for racial equality
Pressed on achieve impossible goals
Nubian eyes let your story unfold
Yes, when they said, "Negros" could not strive
To become educated and emulated
Now we march with college degrees in hand
Thanking God for His plan formulated
Through suffering and shame
Through the storms and the rain
They fought the good fight
Until they boarded that glory train
So, hold your freedom torch high
Giving sight to the ultimate prize
And remember those who paved the way
Thank God for Nubian Eyes!

Nubian Eyes

Let your eyes help you find the words below.

```
S  I  M  E  T  A  M  I  T  L  U  E  X  E  C  A  R  M
E  G  L  O  R  Y  U  T  W  K  B  T  I  P  G  S  A  O
E  P  O  H  D  P  I  M  A  V  F  N  C  M  I  T  C  Y
E  S  T  C  E  B  E  F  R  E  E  D  O  M  T  L  M  T
V  E  O  J  T  S  F  N  U  B  I  A  N  U  O  Q  N  I
L  Y  R  X  A  T  O  M  W  U  O  F  X  N  P  U  D  L
G  E  C  E  E  R  R  E  T  R  A  I  N  T  O  W  S  A
S  H  H  P  R  U  M  D  S  I  G  H  T  E  M  D  U  U
J  A  A  D  T  G  U  U  Y  L  G  L  O  R  Y  E  E  Q
O  I  D  E  S  G  L  C  R  V  U  I  I  E  N  T  C  E
N  L  I  R  I  L  A  A  O  K  C  K  E  E  X  A  A  O
F  P  G  Y  M  E  T  T  T  S  O  U  L  F  U  L  R  F
M  S  R  A  E  T  E  E  S  S  A  V  I  N  G  U  G  M
O  D  E  D  V  J  D  D  J  E  Z  I  R  P  S  M  C  O
E  L  G  Y  U  S  N  E  V  A  E  H  P  S  M  E  U  F
```

Struggle Equality Soulful Ultimate Nubian Heavens
Saving Grace Glory Story Hope Torch Glory Tears
Formulated Freedom Educated Emulated Mistreated
Race Pain Prize Sad Sight Train Eyes

Reflections of a Dream

Do you remember Martin's Dream of racial equality?
Those nonviolent marches
That divine unity
Remember the civil rights struggle
Their blood, sweat, and tears
Bombs, dogs, and water hoses
Their hurt, pain, and fears
Think back to the day
When you heard the news
Oh, the shock and devastation
What a good man to lose
Yes, King had a dream
While he sang the freedom song
He pressed toward the mark
Until he was called home
Now reflect on your dreams
Are you taking a stand?
Against spiritual injustice
Are you holding God's hand?
Dare to dream of better days
When hate is washed away
And faith, hope, and love
Is shown everyday
Tomorrow is not promised
Martin would agree
It's time to get it right
We need spiritual unity
Let go and let God
Erase the pain of the past
When the healing begins
We can live in peace
And finally say
Free at Last!

Heavenly Feast

Feast on the Bread of Life
Sent down from God above
Heavenly morsels of grace and mercy
Smothered in agape love
Feast on God's anointing
Spread like icing on a cake
To restore our weary souls
As He orders every step we make
Feast on faith, hope, and love
The spices for perfect peace
Mix in some Holy Ghost praise
And watch blessings increase
Oh, taste and see that the Lord is good
A feast for your mind, body, and soul
Sprinkled with salvation and
When the meal is complete
Heaven is yours to behold!

Tis the Season

'Tis the season
For positive reflection
Depression rejection
Divine direction
Focus not on your trials
They were made to overcome
Be thankful for your blessings
The gift of God's son
'Tis the season to be joyful
And have perfect peace on earth
Because the reason for this season
Is to celebrate Jesus' birth
So, come all ye faithful
Let us spread some holiday cheer
Wishing you a very Merry Christmas
And a prosperous New Year!